The KidHaven Science Library

The Extinction of the Dinosaurs

by Don Nardo

KIDHAVEN PRESS
An imprint of Thomson Gale, a part of The Thomson Corporation

THOMSON
™
GALE

Detroit • New York • San Francisco • San Diego • New Haven, Conn.
Waterville, Maine • London • Munich

© 2005 Thomson Gale, a part of The Thomson Corporation.

Thomson and Star Logo are trademarks and Gale and KidHaven Press are registered trademarks used herein under license.

For more information, contact
KidHaven Press
27500 Drake Rd.
Farmington Hills, MI 48331-3535
Or you can visit our Internet site at http://www.gale.com

LIBRARY OF CONGRESS CATALOGING-IN-PUBLICATION DATA

Nardo, Don, 1947–
    The extinction of the dinosaurs / by Don Nardo.
        p. cm.—(KidHaven science library)
    Includes bibliographical refrerences and index.
    ISBN 0-7377-2637-7 (lib. bdg. : alk. paper)
    1. Dinosaurs—Juvenile literature. 2. Extinction (Biology)—Juvenile literature.
I. Title. II. Series.
    QE861.6.E95N37 2004
    567.9—dc22

                                                                    2004017273

Printed in the United States of America

Contents

Chapter 1

Discovering Dinosaurs and Their Extinction

Huge and terrifying monsters once roamed and ruled the Earth. Long before human civilization arose, plant-eating dinosaurs weighing thirty or more tons (metric tons) shook the ground when they walked. They were hunted and sometimes caught and eaten by meat eaters with long, razor-sharp teeth. It is no wonder that the first scientists who examined the remains of these awesome creatures called them dinosaurs, meaning "terrible lizards."

In studying dinosaurs, those early scientists also stumbled on a strange and perplexing mystery. Evidence from ancient rocks and other sources showed that the dinosaurs had all died out, or become extinct, at about the same time. The "great dying," as it is sometimes called, occurred more than 60 **million** years before humans came to be. Moreover, the dinosaurs did not meet their doom alone. At least 70 percent of all animal and plant

species on the planet died with them. Scientists wondered what could have caused such a huge catastrophe.

The First Two Great Dinosaur Mysteries

The question of how the dinosaurs died occupied scientists for more than a century. But this was not the only mystery surrounding these ancient beasts.

A meat-eating dinosaur attacks a plant eater. For many years the bones of dinosaurs puzzled scientists.

For many years scientists puzzled over what sort of animal a dinosaur might be. At first, they assumed the bones were the remains of large versions of known animal species. Only later did it become clear that dinosaurs belonged to a unique and unusual class of creatures that existed long ago.

This opened debate on yet another mystery. That mystery involved the concept of extinction. The idea of animal species existing for long periods of time and then dying out was at first unacceptable to scientists. People had been finding **fossil** bones fairly regularly since the 1500s. But before the 1800s, scholars assumed these were simply the remains of previously unknown existing species. The general view was that members of these species might still be living in unexplored areas of the world. Other scientists explained away such fossils as fragments of freaks. These were thought to be deformed versions of ordinary creatures.

Science and Religion

The idea of extinction simply did not fit with religious views of the time. Before the 1800s, most people living in Europe and the Americas accepted the Bible's version of the origins of living things. This was that God had created plants, animals, and humans in a few days. One passage in the Bible reads: "Whatsoever God doeth, it shall be forever. Nothing can be put to it, nor anything taken from

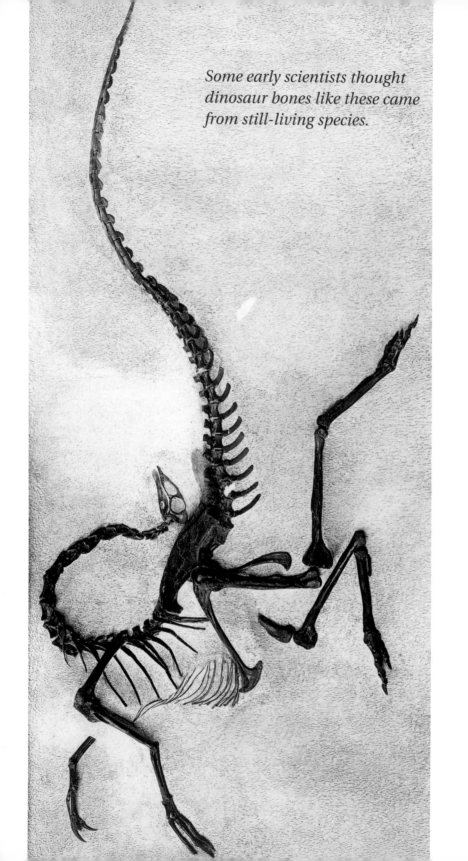

Some early scientists thought dinosaur bones like these came from still-living species.

it." This seemed to say that everything God had created, including animals, had been made to last forever. Therefore, animals could not become extinct.

Early scientists also had trouble accepting the concept of extinction because they did not know how ancient Earth really is. Again, religion and the Bible played a key role. In 1650, James Ussher, a Protestant bishop, made a study of the people mentioned in the Bible. From the lengths of their generations, he calculated that God's creation had taken place in the year 4004 B.C., less than six thousand years before Ussher's own time. In that case, scientists reasoned, dinosaur fossils could not be very old. So there could not have been enough time for nature to cause the dinosaurs to become extinct.

"Swept Out of Existence"

Toward the end of the 1700s, however, the widely accepted view of a young Earth began to change. As time went on, scientists found increasing and convincing evidence that the planet is very old. They also uncovered a great deal of evidence that extinction was a natural and widely occurring process.

A big breakthrough came in 1796 when a noted French scientist, Baron Georges Cuvier publicly stated his belief in this process. He cited the recent discovery of the remains of a smaller version of modern horses. Cuvier also pointed to fossil bones of elephants that were very different from the

bones of modern elephants. These were not freaks, he said. They were members of exotic species that had roamed the world long ago and eventually disappeared.

Cuvier also commented on the discovery of fossils of large reptiles. One of these, which scientists dubbed *Mosasaurus*, had lived in the sea millions of years ago, he said. Another set of fossils Cuvier examined belonged to an ancient flying reptile. He called it *Pterodactyl*, meaning "wing finger." In total, Cuvier said, 90 of the 150 animal species whose fossils had been found in France had gone extinct.

This sixteenth-century painting shows God creating the various animal species of the Earth.

"Living things without number were swept out of existence by catastrophes," he said. "Those inhabiting the dry lands were engulfed by deluges [floods]. Others whose home was in the waters perished when the sea bottom suddenly became dry land."[1]

In the years that followed, a number of scientists and other educated people became interested in

A giant alligator threatens a dinosaur. Unlike alligators, dinosaurs did not drag their bellies along the ground.

giant extinct reptiles. They collected fossils found earlier and organized digs that uncovered many new ones. In 1822, an English doctor, Gideon Mantell, found and closely examined some fossilized teeth. They looked to him like those of modern iguana lizards, only much larger. So he named the original owner of the teeth *Iguanodon*, or "iguana tooth." Mantell estimated that the creature had been about forty feet (12 meters) long.

The fossils of other large ancient reptiles continued to surface. In 1841, a widely respected scientist named Richard Owen provided a general name for these creatures. He called them dinosaurs. He concluded that dinosaurs were a special and specific kind of animal. First, they lived on land. Second, they walked upright and off the ground, like mammals. This is different from modern lizards, which drag their bellies on the ground.

Most important, all dinosaurs had become extinct. For some 160 million years they had been the dominant animal group on the planet. Then, about 65 million years ago, they vanished.

Paleontologists, scientists who study ancient life, mark the great dying as the end of the **Mesozoic era** (the era of "middle life"). Evidence from underground layers of rock and dirt, or geological **strata**, show clearly that the Mesozoic world was filled with dinosaurs. But the strata above the Mesozoic layer show no evidence of dinosaur fossils.

This could mean only one thing. Hundreds of dinosaur species had disappeared from the face of the Earth. The extinction had seemingly occurred in fewer than a million years, perhaps in only a few thousand or a few hundred. In geological terms that is a mere instant (since the Earth is several **billion** years old). What could have killed off so many species so quickly? These nagging riddles of the dinosaurs' doomsday were destined to haunt several generations of scientists.

Chapter 2

Early Theories for the Dinosaurs' Demise

Back in the 1800s, dinosaur hunting was still a new pastime. And the discovery of each new dinosaur species greatly excited scientists and other dinosaur enthusiasts. To their delight, they found that dinosaurs came in many different sizes and shapes. Some were larger than houses, while others were no bigger than chickens. Some dinosaurs had flat teeth for grinding up plants. Others had pointed teeth for ripping and chewing the flesh of other dinosaurs.

One thing that all of these prehistoric creatures had in common, researchers found, was the way they had died. All of the dinosaurs had died out at about the same time, roughly 65 million years ago. Scientists were eager to know how the great dying had occurred. At first, most simply assumed that Baron Cuvier had been right. He thought that one or more ancient disasters had wiped out the dinosaurs.

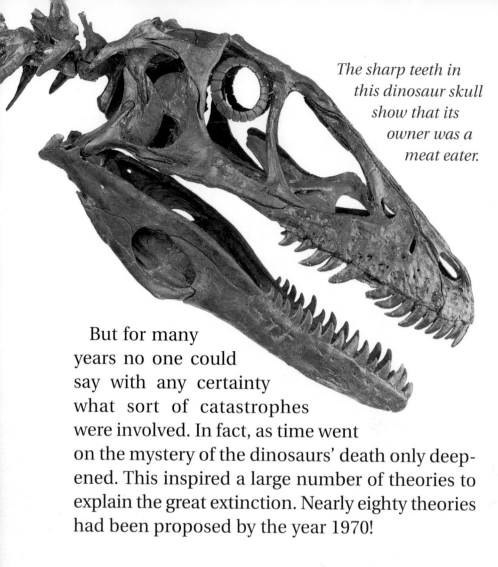

The sharp teeth in this dinosaur skull show that its owner was a meat eater.

But for many years no one could say with any certainty what sort of catastrophes were involved. In fact, as time went on the mystery of the dinosaurs' death only deepened. This inspired a large number of theories to explain the great extinction. Nearly eighty theories had been proposed by the year 1970!

Biological Explanations

Some of these theories proposed **biological** causes for the dinosaurs' demise. (A biological cause is one related to the physical traits or abilities of living things.) For example, one early theory suggested that small, ratlike mammals crawled into unguarded dinosaur nests. The mammals then ate the eggs. Over time, the dinosaurs could not lay new eggs

quickly enough to survive. Little by little the dinosaurs went extinct.

Another theory proposed that the dinosaurs died out because their bodies became huge while their brains stayed tiny. After a while, their brains could not control their giant bodies. In a way, they became too "stupid" to survive.

Still another biological explanation for the great dying was a deadly disease. According to this view, a terrible illness struck a few dinosaurs. It then spread to the others, and within a few years all the dinosaurs were dead.

One theory to explain dinosaur extinction suggested that mammals ate dinosaur eggs like these.

Over time, a number of scientists had serious problems with all these theories. The egg-eating hypothesis was doubtful because it was by no means certain that all dinosaurs laid eggs. So even if egg eaters had wiped out many dinosaur species, some would have survived. Also, mammals consuming dinosaur eggs did not explain how so many sea creatures and plant species died along with the dinosaurs. Similarly, the fatal stupidity of some dinosaurs would not account for the mass deaths of sea animals and plants. As for the disease theory, biologists decided that the existence of a "super-

Some theories of dinosaur extinction did not explain how sea creatures like this one went extinct.

Another theory proposed that climate changes killed Brachiosaurus *(pictured) and other dinosaurs.*

bug" that could kill all kinds of life—land animals, sea creatures, and plants—was highly unlikely.

Changing Climate

A second group of theories about the dinosaurs' demise involved changes in climate. One idea was that toward the end of the Mesozoic era Earth's weather got much cooler. The dinosaurs were used to a warm, tropical climate. They simply could not cope with the cold weather.

A photo shows swirling gases in a supernova's blast wave.

A number of scientists found this idea unconvincing. First, they said, the weather was not the same all over the world throughout the Mesozoic era. It was cool in some regions and warm or hot in others. In addition, during the 160 million years that dinosaurs ruled the planet, some species managed to adapt to each kind of climate. For example, recently discovered evidence shows that some dinosaurs lived in cold areas near Earth's North Pole and South Pole.

Cosmic Calamities?

Some of the most interesting explanations for the great dying are those that suggest the agent of death came from beyond Earth. The vast universe in which our planet resides is sometimes called the cosmos. So these can be called **cosmic** theories. One popular cosmic theory appeared in 1956. A leading Russian astronomer, Joseph Shklovsky, said that the dinosaurs might have been the victims of a

supernova. This is one of the most destructive events in all of nature. Occasionally a star (like the Sun) becomes unstable. Eventually it explodes, releasing a tremendous burst of energy. That energy takes the form of light, heat, and fast-moving, very destructive tiny particles.

In Shklovsky's view, a star located fairly close to the Sun might have exploded 65 million years ago. If so, the blast wave of particles it unleashed would have struck Earth with deadly effects. Some dinosaurs and other creatures would have been killed immediately. Others would have become sick and died over the course of a few years. The reason many mammals survived, Shklovsky said, was that they burrowed underground. There, layers of dirt protected them from the deadly particles.

The trouble with Shklovsky's supernova theory was a lack of evidence. Scientists pointed out that an intense shower of lethal particles would leave "fingerprints" in rocks all over the planet. In other words, some of the particles

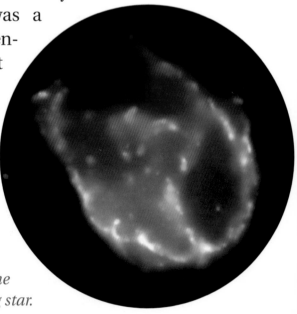

A telescopic view shows the remnants of an exploding star.

would still be in the rocks. But tests made of rocks across the world show no trace of these particles.

Another dinosaur killer from space suggested by some scientists was a cosmic dust cloud. Astronomers know that large clouds of dark dust and small rocks routinely move through outer space. Perhaps 65 million years ago such a cosmic cloud passed near the Sun. Earth entered the cloud, and the dust blocked sunlight for months or years. That made the planet suddenly turn very cold and killed most plants. The plant-eating dinosaurs soon died, followed by the meat eaters, which lived on the plant eaters.

No evidence for large amounts of cosmic dust has been found, however. In fact, for a long time no single theory for the dinosaurs' death was convincing to a majority of scientists. None of these ideas seemed to account for the demise of so many different animal and plant species worldwide. Some scientists actually began to think that no one would ever figure out what killed the dinosaurs. But as more recent history has shown, they were wrong.

Chapter 3

Death by Cosmic Collision

During the twentieth century, theories attempting to explain the extinction of the dinosaurs sprouted like weeds in a neglected garden. Some theories of cosmic causes, such as the exploding star and the cloud of space dust, could not be supported. But the idea of a cosmic event causing the extinction of the dinosaurs did not fade away.

In 1973, Nobel Prize–winning scientist Harold Urey suggested that a large comet (a hunk of rock and ice floating through space) might have struck Earth 65 million years ago. Urey admitted that he had no hard evidence to back up the idea. So most other scientists paid little attention to it.

Only a few years later, however, strong evidence for just such a cosmic collision began to emerge. Most scientists today believe the deadly effects of the impact of a comet or asteroid (a hunk of space rock or metal) did indeed wipe out the dinosaurs. The story of how researchers solved this greatest of all dinosaur puzzles resembles the plot of a classic murder mystery. First came the crime, in this case

the dinosaurs' unexplained death long ago. Then the detectives, in this case the scientists, hunted for evidence and carefully examined several theories. Finally, a trail of fascinating clues led them to an unlikely suspect.

A dinosaur observes the object that will soon destroy it and others of its kind.

A Rare Metal Tells a Tale

The first solid clue to the great cosmic collision was uncovered in the mid-1970s. American geologist Walter Alvarez and his companions were examining ancient rock and clay layers in the mountains north of Rome, Italy. They were not hunting dinosaurs. They were looking for evidence of changes in the Earth's magnetic field.

At one point, the researchers focused their attention on the clay layer marking the slice of time when the dinosaurs disappeared. Scientists call this the K-T boundary. Alvarez and the others wanted to know how long the debris in the K-T boundary layer took to accumulate. So they asked Alvarez's father for help. Luis Alvarez, a Nobel Prize–winning scientist, suggested using sensitive devices to measure the amount of **iridium** in the clay.

Iridium is a metal that is very rare on Earth's surface. It is more common in outer space, however. And over time, tiny amounts of iridium, mixed in with space dust, drift down through the planet's atmosphere and gather in the soil and seafloors. The approximate rate of this process was already known. So, Luis Alvarez said, the researchers should test the clay found in Italy and measure the amount of iridium in it. That way it might be possible to estimate how long it took for the clay to accumulate.

The results of the tests were startling. The clay at the K-T boundary contained at least thirty times

more iridium than would have been expected under normal conditions! Walter and Luis Alvarez knew that the iridium could have come only from space. This meant that a huge amount of iridium had showered Earth at about the same time that the dinosaurs died out. The most likely source was a large comet or asteroid that exploded on impact.

The Smoking Gun

In this way, the Alvarezes suddenly found themselves in the middle of the ongoing debate about how the dinosaurs went extinct. They proposed that when the giant object from space hit Earth, it smashed huge amounts of rock into dust. This dust entered the atmosphere and blocked sunlight for a long time. Walter Alvarez later wrote:

> There would be so much dust in the air that it would get dark all around the world. With no sunlight, plants would stop growing, the whole **food chain** would collapse, and the result would be a mass extinction.[2]

Walter and Luis Alvarez published their theory in the respected journal *Science* in June 1980. At first, most scientists were not very enthusiastic about it. In particular, the critics pointed out, the Alvarezes had not produced a "smoking gun." In detective stories, a smoking gun is positive physical proof linking a weapon to a murder. In this case, the smoking gun would be the giant crater created by

the object when it hit Earth. No large crater dated to the time of the dinosaurs' extinction had yet been found, however.

Researchers hunted for the impact crater throughout the 1980s. The Alvarezes estimated that the cosmic killer was 6 to 10 miles (9 to 16 kilometers) across and would have blasted out a crater 100 to 120 miles (160 to 193 kilometers) across. In 1991,

An illustration shows what the Earth's surface may have looked like after the impact.

the existence of a suspect crater of that size was finally confirmed. It lies partly submerged in the seabed under the coast of the Yucatán peninsula, in eastern Mexico. Scientists dubbed it Chicxulub, meaning "tail of the devil" in the language of the local native people.

The gigantic fireball ignited by the impact expands in this artist's view.

A Chain Reaction of Calamities

Both before and after the discovery of the crater, scientists found a great deal of other evidence supporting the impact theory. Those who accept it have pieced together a likely picture of what happened 65 million years ago. In their view, the impact was fairly straightforward. A giant hunk of space debris smashed into Earth's surface. That event (now referred to as the **K-T event**) set in motion a complex series of disasters that wiped out almost all life on the planet.

In the last moments before the fatal impact, the dinosaurs had no warning of their impending death. The deadly object hurtled toward the planet as fast as forty miles (64 kilometers) per second. It plunged through the planet's atmosphere in an instant and smashed into the shallow seabed on the Mexican coast.

The energy released in the explosion was billions of times greater than the force of a nuclear bomb blast. As a result, the immediate effects of the blast were stupendous in size and scope. A monstrous fireball expanded outward from the impact point. Its top blasted its way through the atmosphere and into space. At the same time, the fireball gouged out a crater 10 miles (16 kilometers) deep and more than 100 miles (160 kilometers) wide. Meanwhile, an enormous shock wave rushed outward through the air in all directions. It was followed by a shock wave in the ground. This one created earthquakes

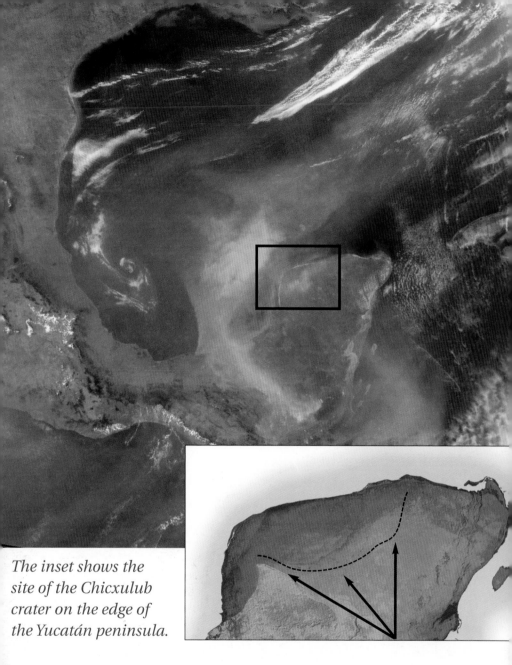

The inset shows the site of the Chicxulub crater on the edge of the Yucatán peninsula.

hundreds of times more powerful than any ever witnessed by humans. In the space of a few minutes, these shock waves killed all living things within 2,000 miles (3,220 kilometers) of the impact site.

The Extinction of the Dinosaurs

Though devastating, more horrors were coming. The impact created gigantic sea waves, or **tsunamis**, which reached heights of 1,000 feet (305 meters) or more. They spread outward and in a matter of hours crashed into all the coastlines on Earth. Meanwhile, red-hot rocks sent flying by the blast rained down all over the globe. They ignited giant fires that swept across the continents, instantly roasting billions of animals.

A giant tsunami crashes ashore. Waves like this drowned millions of dinosaurs in a few hours.

Flying reptiles attempt to escape from red-hot rocks blasted out of the impact crater.

The Extinction of the Dinosaurs

The long-term effects of the catastrophe were even more destructive. The dust sent into the air by the blast and the soot from the fires darkened the skies. This created a long artificial winter. Temperatures in most parts of the world dropped below zero for perhaps two or more years. Many plants (including tiny ones floating in the seas) died. Large land and sea animals that ate plants no longer had enough food to survive, so they died too. This eliminated the food source of the meat eaters, who also met their doom.

In this way, supporters of the theory say, the K-T event set off a chain reaction of terrifying global calamities. Eventually the dust cleared and temperatures returned to normal. But a very different world greeted the returning Sun. The dinosaurs had vanished. And a few small mammals, which had managed to cling to life in their underground burrows, had inherited the Earth.

Chapter 4

Death by Volcanic Catastrophe

Although many scientists accept the impact theory of the dinosaurs' demise, some do not. Evidence of a big space rock slamming into Earth 65 million years ago is so strong that it is not really in question. But some scientists wonder whether this event truly wiped out the dinosaurs.

Another theory involves volcanic eruptions. In this case scientists are not talking about ordinary ones. In a standard eruption, lava, rocks, and hot gases pour out of the volcano. These materials can be very destructive and can kill many people and animals in the general area of the volcano. But such a disaster is far too small to cause a global mass extinction. Even several volcanoes erupting at once would not be enough to wipe out the dinosaurs.

Only rarely in the planet's history have some abnormally large volcanic eruptions occurred. Such catastrophes are sometimes called outbreaks

Normal volcanic eruptions and lava flows (inset) could not have caused the mass extinction.

of **supervolcanism**. In theory, supervolcanism would produce many of the same effects as a giant comet or asteroid striking the planet.

The Enormous Deccan Traps

For example, in a supervolcanic event enormous amounts of iridium would be released from deep inside Earth. Soot and other materials given off in such an eruption would darken the skies for long periods. And that might trigger an artificial winter and a breakdown of the food chain.

Some evidence suggests that a huge episode of volcanism occured at the end of the Mesozoic era. In 1972, scientist Peter R. Vogt called attention to the Deccan Traps. These are a series of rolling hills in western India that formed long ago from flows of volcanic lava that hardened over time.

What makes the Deccan Traps unusual is their tremendous size. Lava flows from an ordinary volcanic eruption cover a few square miles at best and are 10 to 100 feet (3 to 30 meters) thick. In contrast, the Deccan Traps originally covered almost a million square miles. And they remain up to 8,000 feet (2,440 meters) thick in some places. This means that the eruption that generated them was hundreds of times bigger than any ever witnessed by humans.

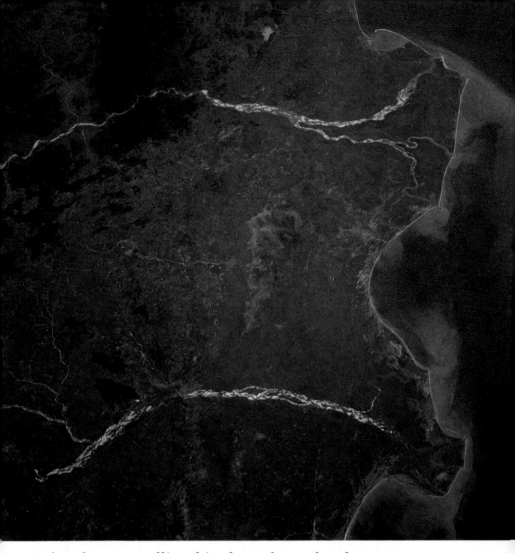

Taken from a satellite, this photo shows the plateau formed by the Deccan Traps.

Too Much Heat, Acid, and Poisonous Gases

An eruption of this kind would release iridium, soot, gases, and other debris into the atmosphere. The amount of these substances would be huge, enough to alter global temperatures. But would it

be big enough to destroy great numbers of plants and animals all over the world?

According to this theory, the eruption was big enough to cause mass extinctions. It was a very long, drawn-out event. The eruption occurred over tens of thousands of years and might even have continued for one or two *million* years.

During those long years, supporters of this theory say, a series of slow-paced but still very deadly

Scientists dig up dinosaur bones in the remains of a volcanic ash flow in the United States.

disasters occurred. Soot and other debris blocked some sunlight and lowered temperatures in some parts of the world. But over time there was also significant global warming. This was caused by the volcano's release of the "greenhouse gas" carbon dioxide. Excess carbon dioxide traps the heat from sunlight and makes the atmosphere warmer. Over thousands of years the great eruption released 30 **trillion** tons (27 metric tons) of carbon dioxide into the air. This raised global temperatures to dangerous levels. And the dinosaurs, along with many other creatures, both on land and in the seas, could not cope.

The eruption spewed out other killer elements as well, the eruption theorists say. These included as many as 6 trillion tons of sulfur. When the sulfur mixed with other elements in the air, it turned into sulfuric acid. This dangerous substance showered the Earth's surface and damaged the tissues of many plants and animals. In addition, some 60 billion tons (5.5 billion metric tons) of poisonous gases, like chlorine and fluorine, poured into the planet's air supply.

The Final Verdict

This and other evidence makes a strong case that an immense volcanic event was responsible for the late Mesozoic mass extinction. Yet the cosmic impact theory also remains very strong and convincing. It is

Whether an asteroid, a volcanic eruption, or both killed the dinosaurs, all that remains of them is bones.

possible that both disasters contributed to the dinosaurs' demise.

Indeed, all scientists agree that both catastrophes did take place. Walter Alvarez, one of the impact theory's chief supporters, wrote:

> The enormous eruptions that created the Deccan Traps did occur during a period spanning the K-T extinction. Further, they repre-

sent the greatest outpouring of lava on land in the past quarter of a billion years. . . . No investigator can afford to ignore that kind of coincidence.[3]

Thus, it could be that the dinosaurs were the victims of a colossal case of coincidence and bad timing. Perhaps by itself, neither the giant impact nor the giant eruption would have been enough to trigger the mass extinction. But by chance both disasters struck almost at the same time. And the titanic combination of these events sealed the dinosaurs' fate.

These dinosaurs are unaware of the comet hurtling toward Earth, an object that will seal their fate.

However the great mass extinction happened, what is certain is that the dinosaurs are gone forever. Some of the most terrifying and at the same time wonderful creatures that ever existed were the victims of a huge natural mass slaughter. Clues to the crime remained buried for long ages. After millions of years, a group of highly intelligent mammals called humans uncovered that evidence and presented it to the court of science. But at this point in time, the final verdict is not yet in.

Chapter 1: Discovering Dinosaurs and Their Extinction

1. Quoted in John N. Wilford, *The Riddle of the Dinosaur*. New York: Vintage, 1985, p. 26.

Chapter 3: Death by Cosmic Collision

2. Walter Alvarez, *T. Rex and the Crater of Doom*. Princeton, NJ: Princeton University Press, 1997, p. 77.

Chapter 4: Death by Volcanic Catastrophe

3. Quoted in Gregory S. Paul, ed., *The Scientific American Book of Dinosaurs*. New York: St. Martin's, 2000, pp. 350, 355.

Glossary

billion: A thousand times a million.

biological: Having to do with living things.

cosmic: Having to do with the cosmos, or outer space.

food chain: The complex system in which sunlight, water, and nutrients are converted into plants, some animals then eat the plants, and other animals then eat the plant eaters.

fossil: The ancient remains or traces of living things. Most fossils are rocklike.

iridium: A dark, heavy metal that is plentiful in outer space but rare on Earth's surface.

K-T event: The collision of a comet or asteroid with Earth 65 million years ago; or the mass extinction caused by this disaster.

Mesozoic era: The era of "middle life," lasting from about 225 million to 65 million years ago.

million: A thousand times a thousand.

paleontologist: Someone who studies ancient life forms.

strata: Underground clay or rock layers.

supernova: An exploding star.

supervolcanism: A rare event in which one or more volcanoes release enormous amounts of lava, soot, poison gases, and other debris onto Earth's surface and into the air.

trillion: A thousand times a billion.

tsunami: A giant sea wave.

Books

Douglas Henderson, *Asteroid Impact*. New York: Dial Books for Young Readers, 2000. An excellent, nicely illustrated overview of the asteroid impact theory of the extinction of the dinosaurs. Aimed at basic and intermediate young readers.

William Lindsay, ed., *American Museum of Natural History: On the Trail of Incredible Dinosaurs*. New York: Dorling Kindersley, 1998. Describes a few dinosaurs in some detail, looks at their skeletons, and briefly speculates about how they died out.

Jim Pipe, *Dinosaurs A to Z*. Brookfield, CT: Copper Beech, 2003. An excellent, up-to-date summary of the subject, this book covers several recently discovered dinosaur species.

Howard Zimmerman and George Olshevsky, *Dinosaurs: The Biggest, Baddest, Strongest, Fastest*. Springfield, IL: Atheneum, 2000. A colorful picture book with more than seventy-five beautiful, accurate illustrations of some of the more fascinating dinosaur species.

Web Sites

Dinosaur Extinction Page (http://web.ukon line.co.uk/a.buckley/dino.htm). A good general

introduction to the asteroid impact theory of the great dinosaur extinction.

Dinosaur Floor (www.cotf.edu/ete/modules/msese/dinosaur.html). An excellent site about dinosaurs for young people, with links to all of the major theories on their extinction.

Zoom Dinosaurs (www.enchantedlearning.com/subject/dinosaurs). This site, sponsored by the WGBH Educational Foundation, is a tremendous dinosaur resource, featuring hundreds of links to easy-to-read articles about all aspects of these ancient creatures.

Index

Alvarez, Luis, 23–26
Alvarez, Walter, 23–26, 38–39
artificial winter, 31, 34

Bible, 6, 8
biological causes, 14–17

carbon dioxide, 37
Chicxulub, 26
climate changes, 17–18
cosmic calamities, 18–20
see also impact theory
crater evidence, 24–26
Cuvier, Georges, 8–10, 13

Deccan Traps, 34, 38
dinosaurs
 meaning of name, 4
 number of species, 12
disease, 15, 16–17
dust cloud, 20

earthquakes, 27–28
extinction, concept of, 6, 8–12
extinction causes
 biological, 14–17
 climate changes, 17–18
 cosmic calamities, 18–20
 volcanic eruptions, 32, 34–39
 see also impact theory

fires, 29, 31
food chain, 31, 34
fossils, 6, 8–12

global warming, 37
great dying, 4–5, 12

Iguanodon, 11
impact theory
 acceptance of, 32
 crater evidence for, 24–26
 energy release and, 27–29, 31
 iridium and, 23–24
 Urey and, 21

iridium
  from cosmic impact,
    23–24
  from supervolcanic
    event, 34, 35

K-T boundary, 23–24
K-T event, 27

mammals, 14–15, 16
Mantell, Gideon, 11
Mesozoic era, 12, 18
Mosasaurus, 9

poisonous gases, 37
Pterodactyl, 9

religion, 6, 8

Science (journal), 24
sea waves, 29

Shklovsky, Joseph,
  18–19
sulfur, 37
supernova theory,
  18–20
supervolcanism, 32,
  34–39

tsunamis, 29

Urey, Harold, 21
Ussher, James, 8

Vogt, Peter R., 34
volcanic eruptions, 32,
  34–39

winter, artificial, 31, 34

Yucatán peninsula
  (Mexico), 26

Picture Credits

About the Author

In addition to his acclaimed volumes on ancient civilizations, historian Don Nardo has published several books on scientific topics, among them *Germs*, *Cloning*, *Gravity*, *The Solar System*, *The Moon*, *Comets and Asteroids*, and *Extraterrestrial Life*. Mr. Nardo lives with his wife Christine in Massachusetts.